SALES LETTER FOR BEGINNERS

A STEP BY STEP GUIDE IN SALES LETTER CRAFTING FOR BEGINNERS

By

Gray Roberts

All rights reserved. No part of this publication may be reproduced, distributed, or transmitted in any form or by any means, including photocopying, recording, or other electronic or mechanical methods, without the prior written permission of the publisher, except in the case of brief quotations embodied in critical reviews and certain other noncommercial uses permitted by copyright law.

Copyright©GrayRoberts, (2022).

Sales letter for beginners

Table of contents

INTRODUCTION	**5**
CHAPTER ONE	**8**
STEPS IN SALES LETTER	8
Identify Your Target Audience First	8
Identify Your Clients by Name	8
Create a Strong, Captivating Headline	8
Create a Captivating Opening	9
Using subheads, elaborate your sales message.	9
You should communicate with the customer regularly.	9
Present a challenge, but ALWAYS provide a resolution.	10
List the features and advantages. Over and Over	10
For simple comprehension, use bullet points.	10
Customer Reviews Are Powerful Persuaders	10
Provide a Bonus to Help You Close the Sale	11
Use your call to action effectively.	11
Remember to Include a P.S.	11
CHAPTER TWO	**12**
ELEMENTS OF A SALES LETTER	12
Customer-centredness	12
Positive language	12
Being simple to comprehend	13
Rhetorical inquiry rhetorical questions	13
Fascinating adjectives	14
CHAPTER THREE	**16**
COMPONENTS OF A SALES LETTER	16
1. The Start	16
2. The explanation or description	16
3. The Reason or Motive	17
4. The evidence or warranty	17
5. Penalty or the Snapper.	17
6. The Close	18
CHAPTER FOUR	**20**
USES OF SALES LETTER	20
The significance and goals of sales letters	20
CHAPTER FIVE	**23**
Types of sales letter	23
Beginning sales letter	23

    New product sales letter — 23
    Sales letter for selling incentives — 24
    Thank-you letter for a sale — 24
    Festive season sales letter — 24
    Request sales letter — 24
    Sales letter for a lost client — 25
  How to Write a Letter Promoting Your Business — 25

CHAPTER SIX — 27
  Difference Between Personal Selling and Sales Promotion — 27
  Personal selling explained — 27
  What is Sales Promotion? — 28

CHAPTER SEVEN — 30
  THE FOUR P's OF MARKETING IN A SALES MESSAGE — 30
    1. Product — 31
    2. Price — 32
    3. Place — 33
    4. Promotion — 34
  How to Use the 4 Ps of Marketing in Your Sales Marketing Strategy — 34
    What Are Some Examples of the 4 Ps of Marketing? — 35
    How Do You Use the 4 Ps of Marketing? — 36

CHAPTER EIGHT — 37
  Conclusion — 37

INTRODUCTION

In the absence of a salesperson, a sales letter is a piece of direct mail created to convince the reader to buy a certain good or service. "A kind of direct mail in which an advertiser writes a letter to a potential consumer," is how it has been characterized. Since the sales letter often advertises a single product or product line, it differs from other direct mail strategies like leafleting and catalog distribution. It also tends to be mostly written rather than pictorial, although video sales letters are becoming more and more common. It is frequently applied to goods and services whose prices make them purchases of medium or high value (typically tens to thousands of dollars). One is a sales letter. A sales letter is typically, but not always, the final step in the sales process before a client puts order and is made to make sure that the prospect is serious about doing business with the company.

The sales letter, which often takes the form of an email or website, has been an essential component of online marketing since the invention of the internet. Spam is the term for unsolicited sales emails, even though these emails are often far shorter than a conventional sales letter. Junk mail is offline, uninvited sales correspondence.

Sales letters may be meticulously tested continuously to find the version that works best in terms of turning readers into customers because of the direct response nature of sales letters. Sales letters are often created piecemeal, with various components being split-tested. This enables the marketer or copywriter to validate the best-converting headline, body text, and graphic design. The internet offers the opportunity to keep tabs on extra factors like the email open rate, bounce rate, clickthrough to the checkout, etc.

A sales letter may be one of your most powerful marketing tools since it allows you to communicate directly with prospects and customers, whether you send it out on its own or as part of a direct mail package. What characteristics define a successful sales letter? There are three main guidelines:

1. Beginning with a hook. Start your message with a topic or idea that will get readers interested in reading more.

2. Tell them the truth quickly. List the top two or three advantages of doing business with your organization in a brief manner.

3. End on a strong note. Use a compelling argument to persuade readers to respond to your closing statement.

What length is ideal for a sales letter? The typical response is "long enough to complete the task." Yes, convincing a potential consumer to make a purchase takes longer than just getting him to ask more questions. However, in the high-tech society we live in today, people are irritated with anything that takes more than a blink to read.

Does this portend the death of the sales letter? No; sales messages will still be read by customers. Keep it lean and harsh, though, since they dislike it when you make them work for it. The appearance of your letter is as crucial to your message—some could even argue that it is more so. It should have a welcoming appearance. Prospective consumers form an immediate opinion of your letter as soon as they take it out of the envelope, regardless of whether they have read a single word of your sales message. Readers will receive the wrong idea right away if it is overly wordy.

To have the best chance of being read, your letter should be open and airy-looking with short paragraphs--including some that are one sentence or even one word long. (A one-word paragraph? Here's how: Write something like "I have one word for suppliers who say they can't offer you a one-year guarantee." Follow that with a one-word paragraph such as "Baloney!" or any similar word you want to use. It is a real attention-getter.

Reduce your sales pitch to its bare minimum so that people can quickly read it. This can include removing the words and phrases you toiled over. However, the likelihood that you will receive a response increases with each additional bit you remove.

CHAPTER ONE

STEPS IN SALES LETTER

Even in this digital age, if you know how to write a sales letter, you can turn prospects into clients. You may connect with a wider range of individuals by developing this talent. However, writing sales letters isn't only for direct mail. You may create sales letters for your website, email subscribers, and other marketing materials. Let's start.

Identify Your Target Audience First

Before you write your sales letter, you must be very certain of who your target audience is. To get to know your potential customer, make a list of your leads and who they are. You can't sell to someone if you don't know who you're selling to. Know who is purchasing your goods and to whom you are sending your sales letter and tailor it just for them.

Identify Your Clients by Name

On the exterior of the envelope and in your sales letter, take the time to address your consumers by name. To your lead, a letter addressed to "Dear Mrs. Johnson" conveys far more information than one addressed to "Dear Potential Customer" or "Dear Sir/Madam."

Create a Strong, Captivating Headline

A strong headline creates the foundation for a persuasive sales letter. By centering it, making the text huge, strong, or in vibrant color, you may draw attention to it. Just be sure to use the correct language to immediately capture the attention of your audience. Even with a large, red headline in

100 points, the writing must be strong or your potential consumer may give up.

Create a Captivating Opening

It should NOT be a dull or uninteresting introduction. Make it count since this is typically the point at which a sale is made or lost. Your introduction can pose a query. It may provide a problem scenario, and you would then offer a fix. Just be careful that your introduction doesn't offer the client a free pass. For instance, if you're utilizing a question as the opening statement, ensure sure the client cannot just respond "no." Because they don't have the issue you've raised in your query, customers who are asked yes-or-no questions are more likely to leave. Your mail is discarded when they stop reading it.

Using subheads, elaborate your sales message.

Subheads should be written in a way that they aid in segmenting the text of your sales letter. It's not a good idea to ramble on for three pages, stuffing the paper with words. Use subheads to summarize each part, entice the reader to continue reading, and, most importantly, keep them turning the page until the very conclusion of your sales letter.

You should communicate with the customer regularly.

Use a personable, welcoming tone as much as you can to conncct with your potential consumer. Keep your sales letter's tone consistent. Identify the client's issue and offer the appropriate remedy. Your sales letter will have a greater impact if you write it as though the client is a friend rather than as a stuffy business trying to get the reader to buy something.

Present a challenge, but ALWAYS provide a resolution.

If buyers are unaware they have an issue you can solve, how will they realize they need your product? Write your sales letter from the perspective of the customer. Make every consumer believe they can't live without your goods, regardless of whether they are a great seamstress or you are selling a glue that hems garments in a matter of minutes. In this case, you have the chance to help those who need a fast hem or who rip their pocket but don't have much time to solve the issue. Regardless of their degree of sewing skill, your product enables them to accomplish it. Simply apply a small amount of your unique adhesive aids in getting them moving.

List the features and advantages. Over and Over

You've presented the client with the issue and the appropriate remedy. Stop not right here. Continue listing the qualities and advantages of your product. If you don't maintain the enthusiasm right away, your sales letter will fizzle out and fail to persuade your buyer to read all the way through. What makes your product superior? How will it specifically benefit the client?

For simple comprehension, use bullet points.

It's simple to fall into the trap of utilizing phrase after sentence as an explanation when expressing facts about your product, features, benefits, etc. Revert to the time-tested "Keep It Simple, Stupid" maxim. Instead of using long, dull phrases, use bullet points. Additionally, bullets assist vision rallying ng the page, which makes your sales letter more enticing to your consumers.

Customer Reviews Are Powerful Persuaders

Customer testimonials are a powerful sales tool if you have them. They enable your clients to express precisely what they enjoy about your goods while establishing your and your product's credibility. Reduce the length and include only a few testimonials. The shortest testimonies might be among the most potent. If a testimonial is too long, cut it short so that you don't lose your prospect in the midst of it.

Provide a Bonus to Help You Close the Sale

You may utilize incentives to increase interest in your product, such as a free trial, no risk, or a unique gift. Utilizing an incentive increases the impact of your sales letter on the consumer since you're giving them something exclusive to the recipients of your letter.

Use your call to action effectively.

Customers may learn what you want them to do by reading your call to action. Make a call right away! Before this deal expires, act fast! There are no shops that accept this offer. Get an upgrade for nothing simply for calling. Use your call to action to point clients in the right direction and advance them through the sales process.

Remember to Include a P.S.

Including a P.S. in your sales letter is a wise move. You may use the P.S. to provide additional vital information you want readers to keep in mind as a parting thought, to remind them that an offer expires on a specific date, or to remind them of something else significant. The P.S. is frequently viewed by readers who may be skimming your sales letter. If it is compelling and strong enough, readers could opt to read the full letter when they otherwise might not.

CHAPTER TWO

ELEMENTS OF A SALES LETTER

Sales letters are written to pique the attention of potential customers of the item or service being marketed. An informational booklet might be sent with a sales letter to give further details. Since most sales correspondence is unsolicited, the recipient may not be interested in reading it. The letter's wording and substance must be carefully considered if you want to inspire the reader.

Customer-centeredness

It's crucial to write from the perspective of the reader. If you can see things from your customer's perspective, you'll be more successful. Promotional materials try to appeal to readers directly. They frequently use closer-proximity terms (like "the user" or "the ticket") with words like "you/your" and "we."

Positive language

In sales letters, positive statements frequently persuade better than negative ones. Here are a few instances:

You might say **"Save your hard-earned money"** instead of **"Don't spend your hard-earned money."**

Rather than stating, **"We are providing a 15% discount. Don't wait because this promotion period will end the following month,"** or **"This month, you can take advantage of a 15% discount."**

The personalized and casual tone

Similar to how you speak, write in this manner. This does not imply that the writing should read like a disorganized conversation. A sales letter is similar to having a friendly, informal, yet well-organized conversation with the reader.

Being simple to comprehend

To make reading easier, use short, basic phrases.
Make each word count by saying only what has to be said.
When writing to the general audience, use straightforward language and refrain from using jargon. If you are writing to professionals alone, you might want to think about employing a few technical phrases, but try to limit your use.

Rhetorical inquiry rhetorical questions

Cannot anticipate or demand a response. They are frequently used in sales letters, particularly in the opening sentence to entice the reader to keep reading. Here are two illustrations of such inquiries:

'Do you aspire to buy your own house but worry about the mortgage payments each month?

Are you sick and weary of mailing checks to pay bills?'

Instead, writing a response, a claim, or even another inquiry right following a rhetorical question might occasionally be even more inspiring or convincing.

Here is an illustration of how to add an assertion to a statement:

'Have you ever given up trying to discover serviced apartments that offer personalized services at a reasonable price? If so, we offer the solution to your search for the ideal apartment in the hotel style.'

Here is an illustration of a follow-up inquiry following the original query:

'Are you overpaying for your workplace furnishings? Why would you purposefully overpay for necessary office furnishings when you wouldn't do so at home?'

Fascinating adjectives

Utilizing intriguing adjectives is another strategy for encouraging the reader to keep reading. Here are a few instances:

'Wonderful, cutting-edge conference space with the most recent technology.'

A completely new idea in professional financial guidance for consumers who desire highly individualized services and amenities.

'A sparkling, low-calorie beverage that quenches your thirst and gives you energy.'

Making taking further action sound simple
Use phrases like "just" and "simply" to give the impression that everything is simple to the potential client. Here are some instances of how to emphasize that taking additional action is simple and uncomplicated.

'Call Dorothy at 98765432 and ask for her.'

'You only need to email the form to me.'

'Simply stop by our Times Square showroom.'

The Essential

Particularly for the letter's conclusion, sales letters frequently employ this vivacious linguistic style. It urges the reader to do the desired action. There are five instances of the imperative in these two statements.

CHAPTER THREE

COMPONENTS OF A SALES LETTER

Make sure all six of these powerful components are included in your sales letters, and you'll see an increase in revenue.

1. The Start

You need to make a strong opening statement that will grab and hold your readers' attention. Your viewers are likely to consider anything specific when they first visit your advertisement or website. They are seeking knowledge on a certain subject because they need to find a solution to a problem. Or they are looking for the ideal present for someone. Another possibility is that they are simply mindlessly browsing the internet while having thoughts about how miserable they are or what that gorgeous man at work thinks of them.

It's an "internal discussion" between them. You have to somehow enter your readers' current train of thinking to ensure that they're they become genuinely intrigued and interested in what you have to say.

A strong introduction will grab readers' attention and encourage them to continue reading. If not, readers can ignore the letter or go on to the next website before you get a chance to make your point.

2. The explanation or description

You must now inform the reader of your mission and the concept or product you're attempting to sell them. Here, you should set out your general argument while highlighting the key points and some crucial facts. Giving your readers the background knowledge that will support your arguments will help them come to see the world from your perspective.

3. *The Reason or Motive*

Here, you enter the emotional realm after leaving the intellectual realm. Readers should yearn for your offering, be inspired to donate to your cause, or want to do whatever it is you're attempting to persuade them to. You need to persuade them to follow your suggested course of action.

You must go beyond simply outlining your pitch for this. You need to convey to your audience what good your product will do for them or how wonderful it will make them feel to follow your advice. Here, you may list all the advantages they'll gain by acting in the way you want them to.

4. *The evidence or warranty*

People may still have some skepticism even after you present compelling arguments for your position. They could be worried about saying or doing something they'll later regret. Now you need to reassure your readers that choosing to accept your offer was a wise one.

You accomplish this by providing evidence to support your claims (for example, by backing up your arguments with scientific data or presenting testimonials from other satisfied buyers). If customers accept your offer and are later dissatisfied with the product, you give some sort of assurance that they won't lose anything. They can do so and receive a complete refund.

5. *Penalty or the Snapper.*

Even if individuals are entirely convinced that what you're saying is true and that doing as you recommend will benefit them, you still need to overcome their fundamental inertia. It takes more drive to persuade individuals to take action. They could quickly forget about you if they don't take immediate action.

We should "strike while the iron is hot," according to an old proverb. You aim to persuade your readers that they must take that action. Here's where you create a sense of urgency so that readers will be motivated to reply right away. Make it apparent that they will experience some sort of loss if they don't reply quickly away, whether it be financial or in terms of status.

6. *The Close*

Hopefully, at this point, your readers are motivated and prepared to take action. In closing, you clearly state what they must do and provide step-by-step directions. A very clear call to action is the first thing you need, such as "Call Now," "Click This Link," or "Come to Our Store Before the End of the Month."
Second, you want to make it simple for them to complete the order, ask for a salesman to contact or accomplish whatever the letter's main objective is. Make sure everything is extremely apparent, including the phone number, website address, email, link, etc.

If you've ever read any form of advertisement or sales article, you should be familiar with these six fundamentals, and they make perfect sense. To create anything that works, though, requires more.

If the outcome is going to be effective in inspiring people to take action, the letter writer, blogger, or applicant still has to add one more component to the assignment. It's really easy. You must love something personally to get others to feel the same way. Collier asserts that "getting the feel of your message counts."

An excellent advertising essay cannot be written if the author is utterly dry. It won't contain any life. A concept excites a skilled copywriter or promoter. People are particularly drawn in by the writing when that energy is captured.

The secret to selling anything is enthusiasm. A brilliant marketer may change the game by taking an average commodity and turning it into a specialized item. Today, this is a common practice online. The way a thing is offered by marketers makes it appear to be so distinctive from the competitors and much more intriguing.

Find something unique about your product or service that genuinely sets it apart from the competition, something that makes you eager to tell others about it. Then, you must ensure that anything you write conveys the passion you feel. It receives its vitality from that. Others will share your enthusiasm for something while you are.

CHAPTER FOUR

USES OF SALES LETTER

The use of sales letters is important
Even if exposure is the main goal of sales letters or offers, they are still the most significant type of written business communication. It reaches out to a sizable audience of individuals interested in a specific good or service and converts them into customers. The purpose of this letter is to pique readers' interest in the product, even if they aren't already. The sales letter must be convincing or strong enough to persuade the recipient to take action, starting with the presumption that they may reject the offer. Most of them are letters that were not requested and were written by experts. The capacity of the writer to utilize language according to his aim, which is foremost to communicate affects the recipient's thoughts, preferences, and actions. Persuasion is meant to do this. As a result, sales letters are approach letters that are persuading or indirect.

The most effective technique to reach potential customers indirectly is through sales letters. These letters are a quick and efficient approach to closing deals. No other letter form has such a broad impact or generates such a significant financial return.

The significance and goals of sales letters

Sales letters are a component of a product or service's PR, marketing, or advertising campaign. In comparisons to other media like as television, movies, newspapers, magazines, handbills, direct mail, and window displays, sales letters have the following benefits:

- Personalization: Sales letters may give advertising a level of customization that is not available with other types of publicity or advertising. Additionally, it keeps clients regularly informed about the business, its offerings, and its services.

- Direct communication: Potential clients may get it directly.

- Contrary to television and newspaper commercials, which feature adverts from a variety of rival companies, sales letters do not have to compete with other advertisements.

- Goodwill: By providing high-quality goods and services, builds and maintains goodwill among customers.

- Convenience: Sales letters may be set aside and read at a later time at your leisure, unlike TV and movie ads.

- Cheaper: Compared to other means of advertising, it is less expensive.

- Easy evaluation of impact: Because they are distributed to a predetermined number of recipients who are divided into demographic categories according to age, income, occupation, etc., their impact can be precisely calculated.

- Fast: Sales letters reach the target individual quickly and directly, in contrast to salespeople.

- Greater Area: Postal sales letters can reach remote locations, which is not achievable with contemporary advertising and promotion methods. With little expense, it expands the market for already existing items.

- Orders for a mail order firm are mostly obtained from this source.

- Customer education: it informs the consumer on how to choose the appropriate goods and services.

- Reminder: A sales letter's repeated appearances have the effect of serving as a reminder. It benefits the client to keep in mind a company's good or service whenever he needs it.

- It serves as a salesperson: Where a salesman cannot physically contact the consumer, a sales letter informs, persuades, and convinces the buyer to purchase a certain item or service.

CHAPTER FIVE

Types of sales letter

A sales letter is a marketing tool that companies use to advertise their goods, emphasize special offers, or remind clients of the deadlines for warranties or other premium services. Sales letters have a great deal of potential for helping businesses achieve their goals. They are frequently utilized online as one of the introduction pages for websites or in direct mail campaigns alongside brochures. In business writing, sales letters come in a variety of forms.

Beginning sales letter

An introduction sales letter is often written to present your brand and products to a consumer or corporate client. The opening sales letter not only informs customers of your presence but also describes why they should choose your items over those of rival firms. Sometimes businesses include a trial term in their initial sales letter. The first page of the sales letter should be kept to a minimum. It must pique people's curiosity, pique their interest, and inspire them to stop by the store to purchase your goods.

New product sales letter

Your past and current clients are informed of new items or modifications to existing ones through product update sales letters. Many businesses utilize comparative information to highlight the benefits of new goods versus more traditional ones. The product update sales letter could also contain a unique offer that allows customers to save money on newer items in a constrained time.

Sales letter for selling incentives

A selling incentive sales letter encourages current consumers to purchase already available items. Writing a sales incentive sales letter will require you to generate a lot of enthusiasm, possibly by temporarily giving a discount, rebate, or contest reward.

Thank-you letter for a sale

It's crucial to periodically express gratitude to your clients for their patronage. The thank you sales letter nearly often includes a statement about how much you appreciate your client's business. Keep the letter of gratitude concise and quickly explain that your items are always accessible to customers at any time.

Festive season sales letter

You have the opportunity to suggest your product as a suitable present for the family, friends, or coworkers of your consumers in the holiday celebration sales letter. "We'd like to wish you a good holiday season here at ABC Jewelry," the opening line of a holiday sales letter may read. A small number of tie clips and bracelets with diamond studs that make fantastic presents for that particular person has just arrived.

Request sales letter

Send your consumers an invitation via sales letter if your business is celebrating an anniversary. This letter needs to be written in a way that makes your customers feel valued and like they are a part of the family. In the letter, mention your items in passing and extend an invitation to customers to join in the fun. For the event, you could wish to decorate your place of business or provide complimentary refreshments.

Sales letter for a lost client

The lost customer sales letter is intended for clients who have discontinued their services or have not made any purchases. You should let them know you miss them and let them know about any new offerings or promotions.

How to Write a Letter Promoting Your Business

Businesses frequently explore new strategies to market their goods or services. To do this, they frequently use sales letters that are delivered to current and new customers to promote a certain area of the business. The letter should attract the reader's attention and include clear information about the company. Additionally, it could provide a complementary good or service.

Step 1: Be particular. Start the letter by introducing the prospective client or customer by name. This demonstrates to the recipient how much you regard them by taking the time to look up their name and utilize it in the letter.

Step 2: Use imaginative language to draw the reader in with a product or service you are offering that might address a potential issue they may be experiencing. Use descriptive words and visual pictures to make this letter stand out in the reader's mind.

3. Speak cordially. While describing your products or services, keep the letter conversational. Describe how the product functions and how the reader could benefit from it if it is a new product or service. Make sure each statement is informative and clear.

4. Be succinct. A maximum of four or five paragraphs should be included in the letter. If the letter is excessively long, the reader can become disinterested and overlook important information.

5. Write the letter's conclusion. Asking the reader to take a specific action, such as visiting your store, giving you a call, or visiting the business website, is a good way to end a letter. In the final sentence, provide all available ways to get in touch with your company, including its address, phone number, email address, and name of a contact person.

6. Conclude the message by expressing gratitude to the reader for his time.

CHAPTER SIX

Difference Between Personal Selling and Sales Promotion

Promotion is defined as the variety of actions used to inform potential customers of the advantages of the product to draw them in and motivate them to make a purchase. Direct marketing, sales promotion, personal selling, advertising, and public relations are all included in this. These are all regarded as sales push strategies. Personal selling is a method of advertising in which a salesperson personally visits potential consumers to introduce the product to them and explain its features and quality.

On the other side, sales promotion employs short-term plans, deals, and incentives to increase sales. Other names for it include "below the line activity." There are various distinctions between sales promotion and personal selling that have been listed.

- Personal Selling Vs Sales Promotion
- Comparison Chart
- Definition
- Key Differences
- Conclusion

Personal selling explained

Personal selling is the process of presenting goods and services to prospective consumers and persuading them to make a purchase. sometimes referred to as salesmanship It is a two-way process from which both the buyer and the seller gain.

The salesperson exhibits the product to the customer, describes its features and utility, does a functional demonstration, responds to the client's queries, informs them of the pricing and any discounts offered, and then persuades them to purchase it. The consumer receives complete information about the goods and has the opportunity to personally see them before thethemtheming on this type of selling. Direct visits to customers' homes are frequently made to promote.

Each consumer may get the message independently with the use of this instrument, and they can respond right away. In addition, as the market grows, so does the demand for a certain product. This kind of selling is prevalent in places like saree boutiques, electronics shops, and auto dealerships.

What is Sales Promotion?

Sales promotion is a term used to describe a marketing strategy that aids at the beginning of sales by using a unique incentive plan for a brief time to entice potential consumers in the target market to act.

According to this style of selling, the offer is only made to the clients for a predetermined period and not all year long, i.e. just during holidays, special events, the end of the season, or at the end of the year. It includes all the actions, outside advertising and personal selling, that increase product sales, such as discounts of up to 50%, Christmas sales, an additional 20% off of 1 kg packs, free presents, etc.

Sales promotion has several benefits, including the ability to quickly increase sales and attract the attention of the target market. Additionally, this technique is useful for getting rid of extra stock. The following are the tools utilized in this method:

- Price off offer
- Free Samples
- Scratch and win offer
- Bonus offer
- Coupons
- Money Back offer
- Exchange offer

CHAPTER SEVEN

THE FOUR P's OF MARKETING IN A SALES MESSAGE

The four Ps represent the crucial factors that must be carefully thought out and put into practice to properly advertise a good or service. Product, price, place, and promotion make up this list.

The marketing mix is another name for the four Ps. They cover a wide range of aspects that are taken into account when marketing a product, such as what consumers want, how the good or service satisfies or doesn't satisfy those wants, how the good or service is perceived in society, and how it distinguishes itself from the competition, and how the business that makes it engages with its clients.

More Ps, such as people, process, and physical proof, have been identified since the four Ps were first proposed in the 1950s.

Knowing the Four Ps of Marketing
In the 1950s, Neil Borden, a Harvard advertising professor, popularized the notion of the marketing mix as well as the ideas that were known principally as the four Ps. In his 1964 paper "The Concept of the Marketing Mix," he outlined the many ways in which businesses may engage their target audiences through advertising strategies.
Borden popularized ideas that are being used today by businesses to market their products and services.

Other significant figures in the sector spent years developing and perfecting Borden's ideas. The ideas in Borden's book were developed by Michigan State University marketing professor E. Jerome McCarthy, who gave them the label "four Ps" marketing. McCarthy is a co-author of Basic Marketing: A Managerial Approach.

When the idea first emerged, it assisted businesses in overcoming the physical obstacles that would prevent mass product adoption. The Internet nowadays has assisted businesses in overcoming some of these obstacles.

Extensions of the original Four Ps that apply to modern marketing trends include people, process, and tangible evidence.

The Four Ps of Marketing Are:

1. *Product*

The first step in developing a marketing strategy is to comprehend the product itself. And why is it required? What does it accomplish that the products of its rivals cannot? Perhaps it's something completely new, and because of its alluring look or usefulness, they will be compelled to buy it right away.

The marketer's responsibility is to describe the product and its benefits to the customer.

The distribution of the product depends on its definition as well. Business leaders must have a strategy for dealing with goods at every point of their life cycle, and marketers must be aware of the life cycle of a product.
How much a product will cost, where it should be located, and how it should be advertised are all somewhat determined by the sort of product.

Many of the most popular items were pioneers in their fields. For instance, Apple was the first to develop a touchscreen smartphone that could make phone calls, listen to music, and surf the Internet. In the first quarter of 2022, Apple estimated that overall iPhone sales were $71.6 billion.

Apple sold 2 billion iPhones before the end of 2021.

2. *Price*

Price is the sum of money customers are willing to spend on a thing. Marketers must consider supplier costs, seasonal discounts, rival prices, and retail markup in addition to connecting the price to the product's actual and perceived value.

Business decision-makers may increase a product's price to make it seem more upscale or exclusive. To encourage more customers to try it, they can also cut the price.

Additionally, marketers must decide if and when to provide discounts. A discount might increase sales, but it also could make a product seem less appealing than it once did.

The global maker of casual clothing UNIQLO has its headquarters in Japan. Like its rivals Gap and Zara, UNIQLO produces affordable, stylish clothing for younger customers.
The inventive and high-quality nature of UNIQLO's goods distinguishes it from competitors. It does this by making bulk purchases of cloth while always looking for the best prices and best materials available. Additionally, the business engages in direct negotiations with its suppliers and has formed strategic alliances with forward-thinking Japanese suppliers.

Additionally, UNIQLO contracts out production to affiliated manufacturers. It has the freedom to switch production partners as needed thanks to this.
And finally, the business employs a group of knowledgeable textile craftsmen who it deploys to partner companies across the world to ensure quality. Once a week, production supervisors go to the plants to fix quality issues.

3. *Place*

Place refers to the location of the product, including its availability online and in physical stores, as well as how it will be exhibited.

The choice is crucial: Luxury cosmetics manufacturers would prefer to have their products sold in Sephora and Neiman Marcus rather than Walmart or Family Dollar. Business leaders always strive to put their goods in front of customers who are most inclined to purchase them.

This entails placing a product solely at selected retailers and ensuring that it is attractively presented.

The term "placement" also refers to marketing a product in the appropriate medium to attract customers.

For instance, the 1995 film GoldenEye, the 17th in the James Bond film series, was the first to not have an Aston Martin vehicle. Pierce Brosnan, who plays Bond, climbed into a BMW Z3. BMW got 9,000 orders for the Z3 the month after the movie debuted, even though it wasn't distributed until months after it had left theaters.

4. *Promotion*

Consumers are to be convinced that they require these goods and that their price is reasonable through advertising. Public relations, advertising, and the whole media plan used to launch a product are all included in the promotion.

To reach their target audiences, marketers frequently combine the aspects of placement and promotion. The "location" and "promotion" variables, for instance, are equally important in the digital era online and offline.

Particularly, the locations of products on a business's website or social media, as well as the specific search terms that will bring up targeted adverts for the product.

Only 10,000 cases of Absolut vodka were marketed in Sweden in 1980. The firm sold 4.5 million cases by the year 2000, in part because of its well-known advertising campaign. The brand's iconic bottle was fashioned in the campaign's visuals as a variety of fantastical objects, such as a bottle with a halo, a bottle made of stone, or a bottle that resembled a stand of trees on a ski slope. From 1981 through 2005, the Absolut campaign was one of the longest-running continuous promotions ever.

How to Use the 4 Ps of Marketing in Your Sales Marketing Strategy

The four Ps offer a foundation around which to construct your marketing plan. Consider each aspect. And if the variables overlap, don't worry. That must happen.

Analyze the product you will be promoting in the beginning. What qualities does it possess that are appealing? Think about other, comparable items that are already available. Your product could be more durable, user-friendly, appealing, or long-lasting. Its components could be organic or from natural sources. Determine the features that will appeal to your intended audience.

Consider what is a fair price for the goods. It goes beyond only the production cost plus a profit margin. You may present it as a premium or luxury item or as a basic, less expensive substitute.

Finding the sort of offline and online retailer who carries your items for customers like you is known as placement.

Only your target customer may be taken into account when thinking about promotion. A hip younger population, sophisticated professionals, or bargain seekers may find the product intriguing. Your media plan must target the appropriate audience and convey the appropriate message.

What Are Some Examples of the 4 Ps of Marketing?

- Place describes the store or location where customers find or purchase your product. Consumers of today may research items and purchase them online, via a smartphone app, in-store, or from a salesperson.

- The cost of the item or service is referred to as the price. set fair pricing for a product, one must consider the market competition, demand, manufacturing costs, and the purchasing power of the customer. Consider several price structures, such as deciding between a one-time purchase and a subscription plan.

- The product a business offers relies on the kind of business it is and what it does well. For instance, McDonald's offers reliable quick meals in a relaxed atmosphere. They might widen their selection, but they wouldn't go too far from their essential values.

- Promotion is the term for targeted and deliberate advertising that reaches the product's target market. To reach the appropriate audience in the right location, a business may utilize an Instagram campaign, a public relations campaign, advertising placement, an email campaign, or some combination of all of these.

How Do You Use the 4 Ps of Marketing?

When preparing to launch a new product, assessing an existing product, or working to increase sales of an existing product, the 4Ps approach can be applied.

A marketing expert may develop a plan that effectively launches or relaunches a product by carefully analyzing these four elements: product, price, place, and promotion.

CHAPTER EIGHT

Conclusion

A sales letter often requires no additional persuasion to convince the buyer to commit to buying the item or service. A unique type of advertising, sales letters are intended to promote a company's products and services. A persuasive sales letter should pique curiosity, inspire desire, and prod the reader to act. Write with confidence and persuasion, but avoid becoming pushy. Give the reader rewards and advantages. Encourage the reader to respond by giving them a call, paying a visit, filling out an attached form, etc.

The goal of personal selling is to enlighten potential customers about a new or current product, raise their knowledge of it, spur demand for it, and turn them into devoted consumers. The consumer receives items at fair prices through sales promotions, and it also aids in retaining clients for an extended period.

The marketing mix, which includes the four Ps of marketing (product, pricing, location, and promotion), is frequently used. These are the main factors that go into creating and promoting a good or service, and they interact heavily. One option for developing a comprehensive marketing plan is to take all of these factors into account.